V&A INDIAN ART DAY BOOK

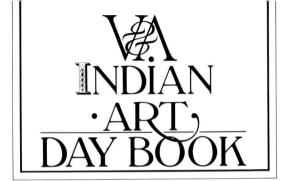

V&A INDIAN · ART · DAY BOOK

Opposite page illustration

NOBLEMEN SEATED ON A TERRACE.
Murshidabad, eighteenth century.

PAVILION
PRODUCTIONS

THE VICTORIA & ALBERT MUSEUM

First published in 1991 by Pavilion Productions Ltd
A division of Pavilion Books Ltd
196 Shaftesbury Avenue, London WC2H 8JL

Designed by David Fordham

Typeset by SX Composing Ltd, Rayleigh
Printed and bound in Italy by L.E.G.O.

ISBN 1 85145 625 2

Front cover illustration:

A LADY WITH TWO CRANES.

Bundi, Rajasthan, c.1760.

Back cover illustration:

FIREWORKS.

Jammu, Punjab Hills, c.1750.

Opposite page illustration

ELEPHANT WITH A MAHOUT AND STANDARD BEARER.

Company School, Delhi, c.1840.

THE VICTORIA AND ALBERT MUSEUM

The Victoria and Albert Museum is the home of the world's greatest collection of applied art and design. Its galleries reflect centuries of achievement in such varied fields as ceramics, furniture, jewellery, metalwork, textiles and dress – not only from Europe but also from the Far East, South Asia and the Islamic World.
The V & A also houses the national collections of sculpture, watercolours, portrait miniatures and photography, as well as the National Art Library.
The Nehru Gallery of Indian Art at the V & A houses a magnificent display of arts from a rich and diverse culture, in the oldest and most comprehensive collection of Indian art outside the Indian Subcontinent.

HOURS OF OPENING
Mondays-Saturdays 10.00-17.50   Sundays 14.30-17.50
The museum is closed for some Bank Holidays and religious festivals.
Ring 071-938 8441 for details.

THE ARTS OF PAINTING AND WEAVING HAVE AN IMMEASURABLY LONG HISTORY IN INDIA, but of these great traditions almost nothing survives from before the medieval period. A few tiny pieces of fabric excavated from Indus Valley sites confirm that weaving and dyeing, at least, were known by 1750 BC. Indian texts of the early centuries AD are full of references to many types of fabric, and we know that Indian textiles were very much in demand throughout the ancient world: classical authors have documented the thriving trade in fine silks and cottons from India, and the Romans delighted in the diaphanous muslins that they called 'woven air'.

The painting tradition has an even more shadowy history. The earliest surviving painted works are the magnificent Buddhist wall-paintings at Ajanta (between the first and sixth centuries AD). Their elegant style is echoed in the later, but also Buddhist, illustrated palm-leaf manuscripts done in Eastern India in the eleventh and twelfth centuries. At the same time, in Western India, manuscripts were being made for the Jain merchant communities in a distinctive style which was to contribute significantly to the development of Rajput painting.

The paintings and textiles in this book, however, date from a later period when successive waves of invaders had left their marks on the local artistic traditions. The most influential of these foreign powers was the Mughal dynasty, which ruled from 1526 to 1858 under such great figureheads as the emperors Babur, Akbar, Jahangir and Shah Jahan. Under Mughal influence, the arts in general distanced themselves from the religious themes that had inspired them for several centuries, and purely decorative elements began to combine with a new taste for realism. Instead of stories of the gods and their exploits, painting began under Akbar to concentrate on the recording of actual events and people. The art of portraiture, unknown to pre-Mughal India, revolutionized painting styles wherever the Mughals extended their domain.

Mughal painting evolved from the Iranian style brought to India by artists employed by the emperor Humayun. Local Hindu artists were soon also being employed, and the distinctive blend of styles for which Mughal painting is known became established. Akbar commissioned great illustrated histories of his own reign and those of his ancestors, but he also had several Hindu texts translated into Persian. His successors Jahangir and Shah Jahan continued the tradition of sumptuously illustrated chronicles, but they were also interested in individual miniatures, mounted in luxurious albums. Provincial rulers too began to emulate the imperial courtly styles, and portraits of *rajas* and *nawabs* at court with their nobles became commonplace.

Regional painting styles grew up and flourished during the seventeenth to nineteenth centuries, especially in Rajasthan, the Punjab Hills and the Muslim sultanates of the Deccan. Highly individual interpretations of common themes evolved in these areas, under varying degrees of Mughal influence. The courts of the desert kingdoms of Rajasthan, whose rulers were mostly strongly opposed to Mughal rule, evolved colourful and bold painting styles in which to depict swaggering Rajput *rajas* on horse or camel-back, hunting, or seated in *darbar*. At the same time, traditional Hindu tales of battles between gods and demons, or of human romance, were still being illustrated in less formal and courtly styles at centres such as Udaipur and Jodhpur. The small and isolated kingdoms of the Punjab Hills escaped Mughal influence to a greater extent until the eighteenth century. Here, religious and traditional themes were explored in a powerful and dynamic style by artists at Basohli and Kulu among others, and stories of Radha and her divine lover Krishna continued to be more popular with the Pahari (hill) artists than mere court scenes.

The grandeur of Mughal painting was only one aspect of the extreme luxury and display of wealth current at the imperial court. Although the earlier emperors Babur and Akbar had been relatively unostentatious, Jahangir and his successors took great pleasure in bedecking themselves and their palaces with the finest ornaments and textiles. The huge pillared halls of the Mughal palaces called for textile hangings to provide privacy and, on chilly North Indian nights, protection from the cold. Textiles are frequently shown in paintings, hanging against white marble walls or over balconies, or used as free-standing screens (qanats) to enclose an area of open space. Whole tents were made for the emperor and his entourage to use while on the move, either on campaign with the army or merely on a hunting expedition. These tents and screens were often beautifully decorated, in embroidered silks on cotton or velvet, in printed and painted cotton, in stamped gold leaf, or woven brocade. Red was traditionally the colour of the imperial tent, but inside it, printed and embroidered flowers would cover the walls.

The palace floors were equally well provided. In summer, cool white cotton floor-spreads embroidered with flowers were laid down, and magnificent pile carpets would be unrolled in the cooler months, often with a thinner floorspread on top. On all types of textiles, the favoured motifs were floral ones: naturalistic flowers, single or in rows, were seen in carpets, hangings and costume, as well as architecture and the borders of album pages. The floral fashion reached its peak under Shah Jahan (ruled 1628-58), whose Taj Mahal, the flower-inlaid memorial to his wife, epitomizes the Mughal style. During the reign of his son Aurangzeb (1658-1707), the floral style diminished along with much of the artistic impetus of the preceding reigns, and was reduced to a small, busy pattern of flowerheads on carpets and the borders of paintings.

While the courtly aesthetic was dominating the top end of organized textile production, the craft traditions of the villages and small-town bazaars continued as they had done for centuries. Provincial courts in conservative areas such as Rajasthan still patronized local skills as well as consciously emulating imperial luxury, with the result that regional crafts were enabled to survive. Some of the finest craftsmanship, however, was found in textiles made not for wealthy patrons but for the maker's own family or home. Particularly in the field of embroidery, decorative hangings and covers or special costumes for weddings and festivals were made by village women using the techniques that had been handed down for generations, and which are still used today in traditional village society.

ROSEMARY CRILL
Assistant Curator,
Indian and South-East Asian Collection

JANUARY

1	
2	
3	
4	
5	
6	
7	

A PAGE FROM THE
HAMZANAMA.
Mughal, c.1570.

JANUARY

8	
9	
10	
11	
12	
13	
14	

WOMAN'S HEAD COVER,
COTTON PRINTED WITH
GOLD LEAF.
*Jaipur, late nineteenth
century.*

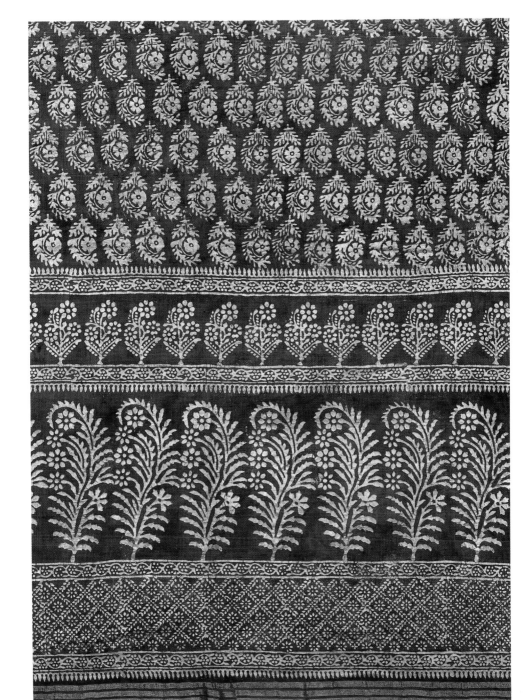

JANUARY

15	
16	
17	
18	
19	
20	
21	

STUDY OF A PARTRIDGE.
Provincial Mughal,
c.1700.

JANUARY

22	
23	
24	
25	
26	
27	
28	

KATHAK DANCERS.
Mughal, early eighteenth
century.

JANUARY

FEBRUARY

PALAMPORE, PAINTED
AND DYED COTTON.
*Coromandel Coast, late
eighteenth century.*

29	
30	
31	
1	
2	
3	
4	

FEBRUARY

5	
6	
7	
8	
9	
10	
11	

A PRINCESS AND THREE
LADIES ON HORSEBACK
HUNTING DEER.
Deccan, c.1730.

FEBRUARY

12	
13	
14	
15	
16	
17	
18	

AKBAR II, EMPEROR OF
INDIA.
Company School, Delhi,
1827.

Akbar II, King of Delhi
And the Prince, Mirza Selim, his Son. 1827.

FEBRUARY

19	
20	
21	
22	
23	
24	
25	

SHAWL, WOOL, LOOM-
WOVEN.
*Kashmir, early nineteenth
century.*

FEBRUARY

MARCH

THREE DUCKS.
Mughal, early eighteenth century.

26	
27	
28	
29	
1	
2	
3	

MARCH

4	
5	
6	
7	
8	
9	
10	

A FRENCH OFFICER AND
HIS SERVANT.
Madras, 1785.

MARCH

11	
12	
13	
14	
15	
16	
17	

TENT-HANGING,
EMBROIDERED COTTON.
*North India, eighteenth
century.*

MARCH

18	
19	
20	
21	
22	
23	
24	

A NAWAB AND
RETAINERS ON A
HAWKING EXPEDITION.
Bengal, c.1775-80.

MARCH

25	
26	
27	
28	
29	
30	
31	

CARPET FRAGMENT.
*Mughal, late seventeenth
century.*

APRIL

1

2

3

4

5

6

7

LADY HOLDING
NECKLACES OF PEARLS.
Mughal, c.1760.

APRIL

8	
9	
10	
11	
12	
13	
14	

MAHOUT ON AN
ELEPHANT.
*Murshidabad, eighteenth
century.*

APRIL

15	
16	
17	
18	
19	
20	
21	

A MAIDEN AND A DEER.

Amber, c.1730.

॥ शागनिरोही चौपह परसविचित्रश्रचीविश्रिरोही तिहुँलोकछविकरुंनछोरी करेंनृस
वागमेंगही प्रेमसुरतिप्रणावतगही सुमैनादमगञ्जएञ्चुलामैं देखिनैंछविनिरुपट
लज्जानै ऊंज्ञीनिकटसरोवरतीर निरमलजलमोनौगंगाधीर सारंगसुरंगहाथनी
दृश्यौ अपनौकरिञ्चापनिकटचुलायो रोह नैंजमगमहैंविग्घमैजियमैपिय
बैराग मनवैरावत्तमृगमसौनौडीठहीवाणः॥ ॥१५॥ ॥ ॥हति॥ ॥ ॐ

APRIL

22	
23	
24	
25	
26	
27	
28	

APRIL

MAY

29	
30	
1	
2	
3	
4	
5	

KAMA, THE GOD OF
LOVE, SHOOTING
A LOTUS ARROW AT
A YOUNG GIRL.
Central India, c.1680.

MAY

6

7

8

9

10

11

12

PARAKEET CHAINED TO
PERCH.
Patna, c.1850.

MAY

13	
14	
15	
16	
17	
18	
19	

CHINTZ PALAMPORE.
*South India, late eighteenth
century.*

MAY

20	
21	
22	
23	
24	
25	
26	

PANEL OF PRINTED
COTTON.
*Delhi, early eighteenth
century.*

MAY

27	
28	
29	
30	
31	

JUNE

1	1992 – Started RT&D.
2	

LADY WITH A GLASS OF
WINE.
*Deccan, early eighteenth
century.*

JUNE

3	
4	
5	
6	
7	
8	
9	

TENT-HANGING,
COTTON WITH SILK
EMBROIDERY.
*Mughal, late seventeenth
century.*

JUNE

10	
11	
12	
13	
14	
15	
16	

A TREE WITH CROWS.
Bundi, Rajasthan,
c.1850.

JUNE

17	
18	
19	
20	
21	
22	
23	

JAMDANI SARI.
Dacca, Bangladesh,
c.1800.

JUNE

24

25

26

27

28

29

30

PURPLE-RUMPED
SUNBIRD.
Company School, Calcutta,
c.1825.

JULY

1

2

3

4

5

6

7

TENT-HANGING,
COTTON.
Mughal, eighteenth century.

JULY

8	
9	
10	
11	
12	
13	
14	

RAJA CHATTAR SINGH,
KOTAH.
c.1870.

JULY

15	
16	
17 ✕	
18 ✕	
19 ✕	
20	
21	Swimming. Louise. 7.15 Pick her up

FRAGMENT OF CHINTZ,
STENCILLED, PAINTED
AND DYED COTTON.
*Deccan, probably
Golconda, seventeenth
century.*

JULY

22	
23	
24	
25	
26	
27	
28	

RADHA AND KRISHNA IN
A MEADOW.
*Rajasthan, nineteenth
century.*

JULY

AUGUST

29	
30	
31	
1	
2	
3	
4	

PAGE FROM A BOOK OF
FLORAL DESIGNS.
*North India, late eighteenth
or early nineteenth century.*

AUGUST

5	
6	
7	
8	
9	
10	
11	

A LADY WITH TWO
CRANES.
Bundi, Rajasthan, c.1760.

AUGUST

12	
13	
14	
15	
16	
17	
18	

DETAIL OF PAINTED
SCROLL.
West Bengal, c.1800.

AUGUST

19	
20	
21	
22	
23	
24	
25	

THE AGED MULLAH.
Mughal, c. 1615.

AUGUST

COVERLET, PRINTED
AND PAINTED COTTON.
*South India, late eighteenth
century.*

SEPTEMBER

26	
27	
28	
29	
30	
31	
1	

SEPTEMBER

2	
3	
4	
5	
6	
7	
8	

THE EMPEROR BAHADUR

SHAH.

Mughal, c.1710.

SEPTEMBER

9	
10	
11	
12	
13	
14	
15	left BT.C D - 1992

SEPTEMBER

16	
17	
18	
19	
20	
21	
22	

RUMAL (COVERLET),
EMBROIDERED MUSLIN.
*Punjab Hills, nineteenth
century.*

SEPTEMBER

23	
24	
25	
26	
27	
28	
29	

LADIES ON A TERRACE.
*Mughal, early eighteenth
century.*

SEPTEMBER

OCTOBER

30

1

2

3

4

5

6

PARAKEET WITH RED
BERRY.
Patna, c.1850.

OCTOBER

7	
8	
9	
10	
11	
12	
13	

HANGING, PAINTED
COTTON.
South India, c.1750.

OCTOBER

14	
15	
16	
17	
18	
19	
20	

INDIAN BLACK BUCK.
Mughal, 1615.

OCTOBER

21	
22	
23	
24	
25	
26	
27	

NOBLEMAN SMOKING A
HUQQA.
Murshidabad, c.1760.

OCTOBER

NOVEMBER

WOMAN HOLDING A
GARLAND OF WHITE
FLOWERS.
*Rajasthan, seventeenth
century.*

28	
29	
30	
31	
1	
2	
3	

NOVEMBER

4	
5	
6	
7	
8	
9	
10	

A HORSE AND GROOM.

Deccan, c.1600.

NOVEMBER

11	
12	
13	
14	
15	
16	
17	

BIRD PERCHED ON A
TREE.
Mughal, c.1640.

NOVEMBER

18
19
20
21
22
23
24

PETTICOAT PIECE,
PAINTED AND DYED
COTTON.
*Coromandel Coast, mid
eighteenth century.*

NOVEMBER

CLOTH MADE IN INDIA
FOR EXPORT TO
THAILAND.
Painted, printed and resist-
dyed cotton, early
nineteenth century.

DECEMBER

25	
26	
27	
28	
29	
30	
1	

DECEMBER

2	
3	
4	
5	
6	
7	
8	

RADHA AND KRISHNA IN
A GROVE. *(Detail)*
Kangra, Punjab Hills,
c.1780.

DECEMBER

9	
10	
11	
12	
13	
14	
15	

PRINTED
HANDKERCHIEF.
English, for export to India,
early nineteenth century.

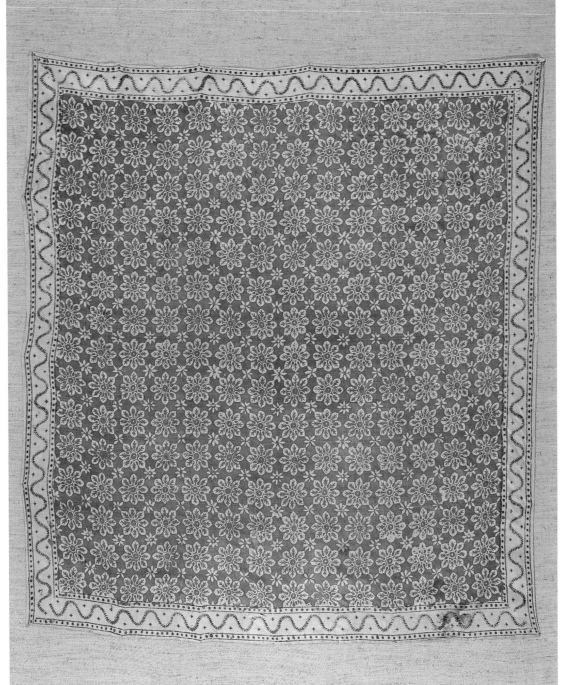

DECEMBER

16	
17	
18	
19	
20	
21	
22	

A LADY WITH
PEACOCKS.
*Mughal, late seventeenth
century.*

DECEMBER

23	
24	
25	
26	
27	
28	
29	

KRISHNA SHOOTING A
LOTUS ARROW AT A
SLEEPING GIRL.
Rajasthan, c.1710.

DECEMBER

30	
31	

KRISHNA AND THE *GOPIS*
(COW-HERDS).
Basohli, Punjab Hills,
1730-35.